M000288924

beaTitudes & Holy Rollers

Jon Welsh

For Barbara —
An art lover like no other!

Jon Welsh
Jan 28, 2012

Undine Press

Copyright © 2012 by Jon Welsh

All rights reserved
Printed in the United States of America
First printed as an Undine Press paperback 2012

The text of this book is composed in Palatino Linotype
with display elements in Adobe Caslon Pro Bold and
Cooper Standard Black

Artwork and design by Michael Steven Platt
and Dianne Aceto of Indirect Light Creative Arts

ISBN-13: 978-0984676118
ISBN-10: 0984676112

Contents

beaTitudes & Holy Rollers

.

Taliesin

Speech of the young poet

I know how many waves are in the ocean,
the distances between all stars,
why the happiest are melancholy,
the number of the world's wishes.

I know unasked questions,
how riddles are made, the fate of fate:
I call the wind on a cloudless day,
I know how many clouds the sky holds.

I am the source of mystery and rhyme.
I know who suffers,
who prays, who responds:
I record the names of God.

My soliloquies express every song.
I am all festivals,
the meaning of judgment,
the measure of eternity.
I gave the Sphinx her riddle,
I put her at the crossroads.

Lament of the mature poet

Once I knew great numbers
And held time timeless. Give me clouds
Waves, winds, wishes - I told them all
And all believed in me. Child I was;
I spoke I thought princely words
Each syllable a beat of blood
But in the silent night I never knew
The counting of tears escaped me.

Ellen's Grief

She's searching for God without belief
returning every thing to its origin
as though starting over would give relief.

She's got voice and presence like a young lark
flown from the nest yet wizened
by a mother's love, the instinctual spark

of wife, lover, partner, friend, the social roles
bees and ants and dolphins and bonobos
live, whose innocence of Darwin tolls

while we toil. We toil at making sense -
every explanation a hothouse rose
in bloom, sent to market; our recompense

dreams of what we haven't got, a star's last kiss,
black dawn rising blue when new skies
show us rosy folds of flesh, our bliss

returning, turn after turn in those we love
awakening, earth rising beyond the moon
knowing no hell below, no heaven above.

Ellen's grief unlike God's is for those things
within her orbit; each day-lily in the field
blooms and passes under the gliding wings

of songbirds or birds of prey, winged ornaments
bewildering our wonder, their beauty and truth
adorning the sky above our firmament.

Auf Den Zug Zum Flughafen Zürich

My return is nearly complete:
I look at the younger muse
sitting across the aisle, asleep,
who yet has fate to win and life to lose.
The conductor has taken her ticket,
Granted passage for our journey
where we are strangers now
and as strangers will depart.

Wiebo I

We are knitting together though we're not old women;
the scarf we're making will warm many people in cold times
when we lay wreathes for our leaders
who sing of endless harmony for all of us.
They would not apologize for our deaths
though we mourn them endlessly.
We know them by name; but we are just numbers.

Modern Birds

I have seen falcons against the sky,
Silhouettes on tufted clouds;
I have read poems like broken-winged sparrows;
Imagined cranes in a distant marsh
    Spelling their journey from the heart
    To the hinterlands and back;
Watched from hilltops geese flying in endless ciphers:
Heard the chatter of these, the cacophony of species
    Against the silent rush of birds of prey.

I have seen full ships sail out against the sea,
    And known the albatross flying along,
Ghost-like in spume and evanescent mist,
    Waiting for a likely spar to light upon
Like foolish lightning glowing on a mast.

An Invitation From The Pope

Tell his eminence with all respect
He has his God; I serve no man's purpose.
Each of us should be so free
that no crown, no mitre, no leader rules.

Tell his holiness St. Peter's Square is his,
and the world's basilicas, tributes to the Christ
who would have shunned such temples
and laughed with Mohammed
were they not crying at the distress
wrought upon the world in their names.

I am honored to be invited, to have such thought
given to my presence that photos and news
would appear to bring an apostate into the fold.
But I have a date with destiny and my audience -
the pope shall dine alone. My regrets.

Prayer

Make of me a tree crowning in the sky
until I am cut down.
Make of me a cricket hidden in that tree,
one of thousands.
Make of me a cicada buried for a decade and more
emerging and shedding my shell
to die, feeding the next generation.
Make of me nothing as nothing I will become:
Let the blue sky turn black and the black sky light
with telescopes' false colors, peering into eternity
as though there's something to see,
something to know, somewhere to go.
Let the traffic roll by in this or a thousand other cities
while mountains stand, glaciers melt
and seas heave their incessant sighs.

Ode to Marble

Hard where I am soft, chipped where I crumble,
stained by dirty air through centuries
while I am mottled by a few decades –
but once turned, fixed, immutable, some inner
vision made visible though eyes struggle
to see who is in that dim mirror
restored and polished, still reflecting
a past brought forward, a future
receding. The tools that hew stone
are too blunt for humans. Interiors
and exteriors don't correspond.
A voice rides the air; its impetus
springs forth while the skeleton
that structures it decays. No Grecian urn,
no priapic stance, no eternal pose,
just a silent bowl that holds my ashes.

The Arrival

Reason lay in lurid orange horizons,
thought's forge cast desire
into crucibles of propriety,
childhood's timber charred at the firebreak,
lightning bolted from coeval skies
cumulating in what thunder said.
I mocked madness, refused responsibility,
stripped innocence, learned at conventions
studied in the streets - mounting debts
until no one would believe
I had nothing, gave nothing, sought nothing.

Monstrous, priapic, leering,
finding no undiscovered face
no legs parted for mine alone
I made figures of imagination
more beautiful and bitter than the rest,
conceived perfection
abandoned the bastard
renewed primal delights
as though sunrise could sequester night.

In darkness I paid the price.

Morning awaits our effortless arrival;
sleep, our slow awakening.

Norteño

Maria Tejano crossed the border with me;
a *mojada*, her chin more finely chiseled
than a novena in marble, her breasts beyond words.

I don't want to ask the existential question—
why she bought that simple white shift, put on
for dancing, a scrim seducing me
with her shadow - there's no answer for that.
Tell me about the broker who bet against you,
whose commission made with a sin of omission
lay in his lies when he said, "It's a good deal."

It isn't your mother's death your father's or mine
but Maria and her unborn child
that I care about. Conflict, inflictions,
wealth and power against labor and poverty,
the discriminations of privilege
I sing. I sing

a land without borders suddenly divided—
conquerors take spoils, families tear asunder,
the land does the bidding of those who trod upon it:
stones turn when they are dug,

fields grow when they are sown, waters flow
and someone diverts them.
Maria's naked next to me, her skin warmly
inspiring. Maria my Tejano lover
survived the crossing,
and now lost in America waits for her son,
new citizen in the northern ruler's domain.
Tell me about walls in Israel, settlements,
taking land from Palestinians whose rights
to home are as Jews. Remember the Rio Grande
where lives flow and ebb and ebb and flow and drugs
cloud the riverbed with blood. Give me niceties
then, against this, sitting in a suburban house
wondering where's Maria, mother Maria
coming to me, for me, looking for metaphors,
the lark, memories of youth, wistful songs,
love forgone, forlorn, spurned by events, poor choices,
bad timing or simply growing old.

Maria's form beckons, her backlit night
drawing me under her veil, downriver
of prayer, testimonials, calls, the *corridos*
singing from every heart not in this room.

Antidote to Frank O'Hara's Excitement

How devastating it was
not to have sniffed gas at Auschwitz.
I never liked petty crime on a grand scale.
Sophie's Choice - Romeo and Juliet
with Nazis and Jews, just another West Side Story.

I missed the tsunami at Christmas, countless volcanoes,
machete mutilations and genocides too many to mention;
millions of cruelties to friends relatives and strangers
by friends relatives and strangers excited
at being alive and giving malice birth.

My body, our bodies, our selves
experiments for chemical combines
cook in the stews of Dow and Union Carbide
while cancer research budgets grow
with obscene morbidity. Fuck them.

Give me tobacco, beads and blankets
and take the damned women away.
In falling light over mesas
shadows climb the arroyos before flash floods
rise from distant storms never seen or heard
words in torrents raging against the light

sweeping kayaks, canoes and sleeping campers alike
along in tumbrels of rock hard truths,
nature brings the human condition
and the state we're in. Real mundane evil

roils in and around us, beautifully macabre,
twisting plots older than writing
perversely chronicled for our pleasure,
each new offense an orgasmic moment,
a story to be told waiting for writers

filmmakers and next of kin to bring it in.
Feels like home, this timeless barbarity,
stubborn, defiant, evolving its own strategies
despite interested parties of all stripes
praying to fictions and letting their demons loose.

How excruciating not to be
at Pearl Harbor or Hiroshima.
I never liked snuff films
not because they aren't erotic
but the ending is so ordinary.

Montage: Wolf Kahn's Landscape

In the arboretum
The near is dense and dark:
Far-off, colors rise, lift our eyes
Leading us on. Evening on Adam's farm.
Shadows crawl from us in closing light:
Man's works at night are dim.
Remembering day
From the far side of the dark barn
A golden square glows,
Revelation's brilliant yellow window:
One turns to see a blue delphinium.

Acorn

I've forgotten comparison to make:
sun, moon, stars, and red or golden flower
slipping beauty's noose, overhung, unslaked,
her legs or his or ours lacking power

to move imagination into action
as squirrels play, chasing up and down trees
leaping bough to bough, their satisfaction
turning the grounded eye of those not free

to wish they could be, muttering lips pursed,
whose fingers till their garden's dirt. They weed —
finding buried nuggets of some lost verse
hidden in pages of a book now freed

to sing again before being tossed aside
a stillborn oak, whose mighty form has died.

Diagram The Sky

Bobbing stars
Speckle fluent rivers

Constellations dance,
Sonnets swirl away

Lands and words erode
Effluent fills the sea

I stand in shoals
Impatient for a boat.

A Life in the Day

January 30, 1969

The man wearing his bowler climbs up, pipe stoked,
watching the Beatles' farewell concert. In California
they're cleaning up Santa Barbara's oil spill
while Soyuz spacewalks start another race.
It's just a day at school; Thursday night is orchestra.
We made love in the car
on the way home, just the two of us, years before
polyamory came into play.
Today Suzanne Williams serving time
for pouring paint on Selective Service files
had her sentence reduced while Smrkovsky
the Czech was elected chairman of the House of the
People with 85 in opposition. The archbishops of Peru
called out a state of sin, called out inequality
as Mr. Rarick, a congressman in America freed
from a Nazi camp 24 years earlier was stripped of his
Democratic seniority for supporting the racist
Wallace.

There are miracles to celebrate:
Israelis are talking about saving the Jews of Iraq.

In fashion we don't know
if it's the year of the anatomy or of the spoilsport;
I missed the party where women wore see-through
dresses but remember the man with the x-ray eyes.
Two Dicks want to record America
though Kleindienst is for careful control
while Nixon wants to fuck everyone.
Not much has changed since
Bruckner's Sixth filled Carnegie Hall
and Sirhan's lawyers fought his indictment
as though Bobby Kennedy never died.

The Wrights announced Susan's June wedding,
lighting up Lexington Avenue
(we made love again fueled by the pill's abandon)
while Brown Brothers, Harriman and Illinois Central
denied that Union Pacific had a controlling interest.
James McGovern died.
Peruvian water laced by insecticide poisoned 300,
and in Ulster they fought over civil rights reform.

At 56, a sculptor of porcelain birds beamed to heaven
and Nero Wolfe of West Thirty-Fifth was denigrated
by Harold Schonberg. I think I remember him
or his cousin Arnold the musician, though perhaps
they're not related.

A year after Tet they're talking about a truce;
the war goes on, an endless reel
whose misery in scene after scene defies humanity
but sells newspapers and fuels the evening news.
Read it, see it, live it; a consumption
that kills the spirit, begging for a merciful end
as the press spins down, the bloodletting over,
ink red and black turned to pulp.

1001 Poems of Lifshin

Her words tie down the tracks,
binding rails leading to each stop;
both origin and destination
singing clickety-clack clickety-clack
no matter what train freighted
with goods or people or raw ore
rolls on by, streaming scenery
framed in a passenger's window
passing Kinkadean vistas and gritty ghettos
punctuated by bucolic water towers
in small towns where not much happens,
where everything happens to be forgotten
the train's whistle dappling the air
rising and fading away.

Basel to Engelberg

The road presses between mountain and sea,
narrow, cut, threaded on sheering rock
near falling water.
Were I literate in a literary age
I would have called it a chthonic thread,
its spool unwinding over and around
white-capped outcrops cutting pellucid pools,
breaking surfaces, thrusting skyward;
now it's on a hoary face bearded by clouds,
wrinkled with asphalt rivulets.
Trees — the stubble of aeons —
define verticals against every slope;
there's some geometry in that geography,
Swiss ruggedness keeping secrets in every valley
marked like the furrows on an aging farmer's face
or the creases of careworn bankers and watchmakers
who have skied glaciers since youth, their crevasses
nestled between history and fate.

Music in the Night

There's stormy weather on the west end tonight
over in the east blues are howlin' against every shore,
horsehairs ripped off the bow
frenzied notes of passionate discord,
harmony and chaos sounding riotous.

Tyrants know nothing of this music,
playing their solos against the misery
of peoples, gypsies and refugees;
we sit in recital with suspended concern
as movements march on toward dinner and dessert.

Tonight is the night of passionate dreams,
schemes for love and freedom,
remembrances of indecorous dances
captured in melodies scored
against the turning hours.

Each phrase sounds a lyric part,
later a coda will describe an epoch;
some voice claiming it as its own,
defining a time for all times,
sowing a seed that once sown
will last and outlast the moment of its birth

singing the joys of childhood, the solace of age
against the blind march of the human heart
beating out its own destiny.

A Solitary Dove

I fly under dark clouds toward blue skies
horizons escaping as I approach;
I rest on grounds trembling, trembling
as I do with fear of flights
leading nowhere but oblivion.

Wings turn against the wind
while time passes and distance grows
between my origin and destination,
the nest I left before I called it home.

Some I seek, some I left behind
and nowhere is a certain outcome
sure to give me rest. I fly,
I fly from what I know
to what I do not know,
both sorrow and hope in my breast.

Fire, Air, Earth, Water

Come now, your legs split
Like a lightning-shattered trunk
Come now, your limbs and storm-frenzied leaves
Uprooted and freed from earth's sodden bonds
Come now after that presence
Whose watery forms heave and sigh like psalms
Reposed where reason is not
In the elements of revelation.

Hospice

The moon with ragged edges descends above naked trees
in a cold blue sky. A southern sun climbs before its decline.
We are all in hospice,
but now you have the twenty-four hour plan,
fresh linens, attendants easing the end
coming when you call or are called.
Let's not think of luck or bad breaks or early exits
from a play with so many acts. The moon will rise
full and orange next month, low in the east
as the sun slides down and lights seek to prolong
the dimming day. We will see you then
young and fulsome, ready to brighten our night
as you ascend into darkness, distant stars
shaping our visions of the heavens
as you pull tides toward us, then away.
We will call each other, remembering you,
seeking friendly care before slipping into eternity.

Distillation

I used to be a classic,
a great book, a model T;
I used to be, well, something
studied and storied and cataloged,
both the slang of youth and lexicon of scholars
but now I've forgotten my name.
Was it Odysseus or Ulysses?
I don't remember if Homer or Virgil
would know any more than I
the best path to Parnassus.
All I know is when I bend an elbow
the barfly says "you're a work of art."
I used to be, that's sure. But now?
I buy another round and troll the indices
of books looking for my entry.
Someone's library has me, but whose?
What fate now surprises me
word by word, page by page, year by year?

A Vacant God's So Torn

One constant runs between big and small —
funhouse mirror ratios, new realities;
the real me emerges as one I can't see
except in time-worn reflections, another's eyes,
folds in flower petals. That blade of grass
a fraction of a lawn, a field, a meadow,
my words neither lighter than air nor deeper than space
or meanings intended no matter which you find.
Intestinal bacteria reach a plateau,
Molecules weigh the world
sorrow by sorrow where joy in God is gone
no matter what lives in believers' guts.
Scriptures in kilos, praise in pounds, a clockwork machina:
when known yet more remains unknown or forgotten.
God is or is not, or we could be pondering
possibilities even Hamlet couldn't argue.
Among billions a holy vacancy
seems likelier than hypotheses
put out by prophets breeding sects
in the names of idols,
their promises and admonitions
as useful as salamanders jumping from flames.
Between belief and math lies the mystic

with curious logic and credulity, whose lure
finds those seeking a credo;
in many dimensions number explains everything
but not all spires rise from the same foundation
or reach toward a single sky.

Goat

There is nothing old about the young
except they will be old. Budding leaves
color and fall; their predecessors wait
mouldering in earth, wistful of airy times
when they once hung on greening boughs
in storms and sunlight, winds changing
as frequently as youth changes fashion,
fresh sprigs beyond my licentious wish
where perhaps fame or wealth might reach
but words no longer seduce.
The economy of eyes is quick –
a glance, a gaze, aversion or engaged
sometimes the shade-sheltered dream
of a picnic beneath leafy limbs in season.
We have come here looking skyward
while lying in soil fertile with age
in the ruts of those before us
who we shall soon become. Let us go then
as quickly as we can from that past
toward what day denies until night comes.

Baudelaire

Winter sun in summer night!
Frigid ice whose fashions –
pale jewel made bright –
rieve the fragile air, whose passions
affront that pure delight
we might have if you were light!
You turn and set and rise
in fire; from the skies
lucid waters recede at your request
and when the placid, deprived of rest
complain, you cry "Where is my twin
the hypocrite? Who calls my sin
a phase? Let the phrases
of your reproach
mark my obdurate approach
and far-flung revolution!"
Phases of the moon,
a poet who sang
a voluptuous rune.

Cortege

I walk entrained among the shades and some,
whose time past, await the bier and fast sleep
of predecessors; professors who come
before the altar seeking mates they keep

beside them in bed, near them in the pew
where hard wood strikes a certain mortal chord
as they mourn, not without envy those few
caressing better the unspoken word;

musing upon their learnéd fate they look
beyond stained glass at indifferent skies,
bent light and dark covers. A holy crook
processes foot by foot forward; their eyes

scan the steps before them lest they slip and fall,
bearing poetry dead among us all.

Digital Nomad

I see your picture in my mind
scanned on the hard drive;
locked in a storage box
where I pay to preserve reminders.

I listen to Nashville songs
written by others that could have been mine –
my poetry on the living room wall,
my thesis lining the upstairs hall

and some days I recall the landscape –
tall grass against the tree line beyond the fence,
lawn tractor, tilling the garden, building the shed,
the tears we used to wash the present

into the past, those days of youth and deceit;
we should have known better
when our first son was left dead
in that dark afternoon room

where the doctor's procedure
killed a marriage as well
and all days after. Beyond the divorce

that unnamed boy exerted such force

I remember without stills
the picture of what went wrong,
the solution you found
in another's arms. It's not long

from now to then, just an instant,
coffee blended from a packet
instead of brewed with time's
slow aromas, tied to that place

where once together we fell apart.

II

Preparing to be homeless in a digital world
means living in the clouds,
in the azure, or entangled in the Amazon
where flora can be as deadly as the fauna

in a shelter in some strange city.
Or on a bus to nowhere.
A fifteen-year-old not prepared
for this wilderness downloads Dad's stories –

they're just bits in the memory
of whatever device he uses.

I sold the house, the business failed
yet dreams continue while blood flows

infused in the crush of grapes.
Email chronicles abstractly a life
with all attachments preserved:
lovers, lies, points of view, the endless slog

through thickets of rational thinking
absent faith in anything but reason.
The laptop goes with me, a better companion
than woman, its silicon synapses

capturing, communicating, and forging links
as though I were in Black Mountain
or Iowa
or Paris, or Greece or in bed

with the French Lieutenant's or any other woman.

III
Conversations skip along as long as there is
bandwidth
for the subject at hand; hotspots here,
hot topics there, not least the recordings
of lyric voices long since forgotten

their rhythms, tones and words
captured and encoded by various agencies.
Nothing much is said: everything is said.
Silence like white space

between words on a page,
in the air as a page turns, a gessoed canvas.
Something is there: nothing is there.
Presence like absence

reduces everything to memory
where what is brought up is put down as fact.

IV
Transformations turn upon this and that
like the net's long lariat roping a wild horse
or a rodeo calf released from the pen
only to be caught and released again

before the slaughterhouse ends the show.
Icons of the future populate locations
that may or may not survive
as we surf waves of ubiquity searching for something

scrolling the results . . . archeologists sifting sand
in deserts of digitization where so much often is so
little.

We're connected to the past constantly
because everything on the net has already happened.

I'm looking for the future through an umbilical cord
tethering me to what has been.

V
Soon the word will arrive. Not the word of scripture
or the fab four, but the final syllable,
one phoneme of utter simplicity and truth
cutting through meaning like a scythe

reaping the sown fields, separating chaff
in threshers, working to make a bite
so the homeless might thrive and the affluent
continue living in silos of comfort

awaiting, as lonely as any other,
comforted by sweet societies
not born of bus stops, underpasses and steam grates
warming the winter night.
I'm looking for my Red Wings,
thermal socks, and foul weather gear
for those days when friends tire of me
or I simply want to be alone.

It's only dental work I worry about.

VI

There's more to it than that: getting the words out,
words written on subway walls
and tenement halls speaking in tongues
many know and many don't understand.

Painted buildings, inked bodies
stylize the message before it's digitized
on some web page, captured in a web cam
or on a chip before it's uploaded.
Yes, there's more to it than ending the reign
of paper, of place, of biography,
storytelling about someone, perhaps a self
not unlike me, a somewhat memoir

written in advance of the memorial,
the processional, the crematoria
and the prepaid domain name
good for a hundred years

funded by the estate of the deceased.

VII

Every bit is fungible and means something different
every time it's used. Moments are recycled
into stories as though they're as true
in the telling as when they were told differently

to a different audience. Frozen words
seek an inner voice to find;
often leaving uncertain
what was said, what was meant

wondering if some critique
would speak to them, brighten the darkness
redeem the purchase of their time.
Against this lies the industry

of forgetting and rebirth
escaping the amniotic sac
bearing memes, memories and the genome,
histories yet to be told

broken into strings of manipulation.

VIII
There is no end to beginning
except to start again from a different place
on the same journey, seeking something
even digital nomads can't find

though they retain endless archives
hoping that reconstruction
will reveal some thing not yet seen,
will remind someone of something not said

wandering anew toward some end,
discovering the final score and its measure,
tuning the voice to hidden melodies
and the heart to a universal beat,

bit by bit making its way toward humanity.

Simplicity

It's hard to be simple. I spend all day
in trenches, digging spondees and dactyls:
once, finding a fig leaf, I looked around
for a statue to put it on (that's my loose
imagination). My shovel strikes time
to music; when my batteries wear down
I listen to birds calling each other,
laughing at us, singing from boughs on high.
Makes me wish, sometimes, I could be a cat.
It's easy to be hard: just complicate
things. Try explaining a complicated
thing. Which makes me, when thinking about
how many are smarter than I, whimper
that it's not, after all, hard being simple.

Kay's Crystals

Lead soldiers melt under matches
a focused glass flames fallen leaves;
icicles fulsome on winter eaves,
birds wheel and land walking
on doglegs splayed in snow or sand.

As the world turns Atlas shrugs
each moment seeking help,
relief from the torment of myth,
freedom from the glyph.

She reads the river of time
crusted on the rimed explorer's beard
confident that in great circles she is heard.

There's nothing like a modest, witty poet
so unassuming she knows it.

Icicles melt into the Niagara.

Smitty Johnson

Smitty Johnson was a good talker, a Pied Piper. His momma always told him you can do anything you want and he believed it. Mostly he just talked. He had great ideas. He could imagine being anything and get others to see it too; problem was he never did it. Was the damnedest thing as they say, the damnedest thing - all he did was talk and it sure sounded sweet as the corn growing up in the fields ready for the barbecue, but it didn't amount to a bushel of common sense. Smitty read those stories about astronauts and presidents and war heroes, watched movies a lot, and listened to records spinning around on the phonograph player his parents had. He always had six bits for the jukebox, imagining that he could make people's heads turn just like those records once he started playing piano. But he played for a few years and then stopped. He talked good, but when it came to doin' his habit was to start and get just so far and then let it go. Damn shame. If he'd picked one talent he might've been something, might've made something of himself. As it happened he sat in this corner bar bending his elbow and an ear when he could find one, mostly strangers after the regulars heard most all of it. Else he sat home bending an elbow and doing nothin' much. After a while he mostly kept everything inside his head. Good place to keep it probably. There was the time, though, that he worked real hard at telling stories. Thought he could be a writer, thought he could write a movie script, tried his hand at writing poetry then put it away figuring wasn't enough in it. Spent most of his time figuring out how to get this girl or that woman into bed. Often came in with someone, and if he was alone coming in often left with someone. Had a lot of success — some failures too — but running the percentages didn't do too bad for himself. Not sure the women felt the same way, given he was all talk, although in bed he had a bit of action, least from what I heard. But their dreams of having something more than just rumpled sheets always fell apart. Smitty Johnson was always moving on to the next thing, whatever he wanted because his momma said you can do anything you want. He thought that meant you could pretty much do what you wanted with other people too. Took a few lumps over the years, but as he got older he toughened up so he pretty much stopped worrying. Didn't think too much about the past; he was always looking to the future. That was one thing you could say about Smitty. Somethin' didn't work despite what momma said didn't matter much. He'd shake it off get up get back on his feet and try something else. Indefatigable — fancy word that someone used once that he kinda liked. He used to throw it off like "nothing tires me out I'm indefatigable." Wasn't totally true. After he'd gotten snockered he tired pretty quick, but mostly he held his own and there was nothing much anybody could say to him. He just did what he did over and over again dreaming about being everything that he wasn't, dreaming about being something although all he was was a talker.

Lighthouse

Light dances through the mist,
sweeping round, warning ships from ground.
Waves break upon the rocks
ironically, one thinks: there's nothing to see.
No intent under currents below
and all the fury and the foam
suggests that one who's here is better home.
Every ship sailing sails alone,
riding swells, facing rogues
that break masts and towers,
wrecking hulls with untold power
and only this is known —
to sea was not a place to be today.
Visions of such storms unsettle the eye—
when skies are once more blue
the mind still roils with overcast hues;
yet we find joy living and looking in wonder
at what's here and not yet sundered
by our final loss
of those who on storm-wracked seas were tossed.

The Miner

Every day my tongue cuts gems
from veins of unspoken sentiment.
Crystals separate from dark seams,
surrounding sediments
shored against the deep draw
keep collapsing darkness away.
I prospect in solitude
a lifetime's labor buried here.

Friends

Not until everyone becomes an enemy
will I find a friend: for who comes
back from that precipice holds with a sturdy grasp,
knowing weakness and strength
alike, holding no illusion. Night hides
in day's shadow; beyond the blue lies black
and silenced birds while crickets sing
until the early morning owl wakes
as warblers raise their cry, calling
others on far-off boughs. A friend calls me.
Forgiveness fetches friendship,
pulls anger out like a rotten tooth
opening a rueful smile
that acknowledges complicity and guilt.

The End

What will be my end? To sit
in unremarked cafés amidst the din
showing crinkled papers to strangers,
or celebrated, fêted, sought for my words?
I see the mural on the wall,
the clock, the mosaic overhead;
in this cathedral of conviviality
silence reproaches those who look
at solitude, a poet's Gethsemane,
yet believe there's less
in many words than a well-spoken few.
A caricature of reverence
begs for recognition but knows
the futility of demands.
One can only ask
what others may give; those who live
endlessly no longer seek cafés for idle conversation
but a banquet with voices from the past.
We are not far from pretense;
I write with a golden pen.

The Berghoff Café

In this café
Where good stout burghers stand
tables tilt under the shade,
linden-trees set against the sun,
drunken breezes,
my smiling waitress,
wine, cheese, lawns, a beach.

Inside the baroque bar:
heralds, crests, escutcheons,
names taken, busts of those fallen.

Of these quaffed pillars
time has its way, wends homeward
fictions full as fact
any other's flesh better.

No substitutes here:
beer and bratwurst,
Kalbfleisch und Bier,
etwas zu essen, zu trinken etwas.

It's something:
cravated citizens
belching, flatulent,
shameless as a hanging man
bone grinding against bone.

This sad café
where I drink alone
calls me to other lands.

Dear Reader

It doesn't matter to me:
are those straight broad blades of grass
reaching toward the sun or are they are bent?
I didn't notice them the first time I saw the field.
Now they become what they are
though it's not clear whether bent blades signify submission
or they've been crushed by animal hooves or car wheels
gone astray and anyway who the hell knows
a straight blade?

It doesn't matter on the approach
to Black Mountain who my companions are –
they are ghosts – nothing's left but testimonials
in these hills of North Carolina where green boughs
black in shadow turn blacker at dusk;
the heat doesn't rise off the highway
but descends through air and sits on everyone.

If you read the woods and slopes
the landscape's text punctuated by paths
and roads, river crossings and bridges
from here to there, as though there's somewhere to go.

Someone marked this land long before I arrived
but it's nothing to me: I'm here with you.

We'll bed down under the trees
or on an open field where our breath
will rustle through windrows
joining the chorus of myth and history
as we fuck each other, turning like leaves
in a quick breeze before fall's dampness
turns us into mulch.

It was Lady Chatterly I learned to love
when the library wouldn't let me check her out
so I had to read between the stacks
until I became her lover. She returns to me
nightly, slipping unimplored in the quiet wilderness
of dreams and poetry into this small hut
where imagination holds a clearing
but wild animals lurk in the shadows.

We build fires, and in the light
love flickers across your face, illuminating
the manuscript of your body as I read its braille;
smoke wends beyond the chimney
leaving its pungent presence
seeping into our mottled hair,
blankets, and books whose covers we sleep between.

Some memories alive, some merely fictions
it becomes harder to remember with each
passage, each reading, each telling releasing
the foxed pages further from what was
to what we want to be.

Thus we end this tale betwixt
a wink and a nod, the absent snort
of one who's fallen asleep on another
dreaming of wakening to a new face in a fresh light.

Nemerov Rewritten

Skaters scribe their meaning in the ice,
characters in style, an unspoken language
written on water that remembers nothing,
neither wind nor wake,
while the wrist's bony constellation
stains the purity of the page with ink.
A bat's echo paints the darkening sky.

The Oak

That stout tree struck by lightning
bore its grim grin, remnant of a brutal stroke
enduring for years, growing wider with age,
revealing nothing of the inner sap
flowing up and out sturdy branches
where each leaf filigreed the gnarled wood
for a season, then fell
to ground; some, perhaps stubborn, stuck to limbs
through winter, stiff and brittle and brown
until new shoots pushed them from the stem
and schoolchildren picked them for projects,
capturing the past in the faint scent
of warm wax, construction paper and crayon.
At a certain age we leaped to the lowest branch
sitting astride it with no upward progress
possible, lacking ladders, ropes, and tools
for higher ascent. We read books, we dropped acid,
yet neither those inner leaves or visions
revealed to us the meaning of that stoic smile.

Strangled Sonnet

On hearing a poet make fun of poetry and Milton in a bad
but funny verse.

Forgive me but I forgot the form —
today's chic non sequiturs escaped me
but that's all. That's contemporary
now, when ennui and discord mark the norm.

Short a syllable, lacking a rhyme
with meter and syntax all out of whack
each disillusioned clique takes a crack,
poetry in small measure though past its time

for lyric angst, lacking influence
over any but the smallest coteries,
edgy or academic wannabes
talking to themselves as though they make sense.

In such times as these, when all lack purpose
what's left but elegy and epic prose?

Late Fall In Celluloid

Words settle on the page, October's umber blackens,
time decays; an isotope of memory
the half-life of love and politics mingled
on acetate. Who wrote the screenplay
we don't know but leaves above and below
reflect the fall as we watch the garden scene.
This old film — its patina translucent in the light,
dark in the dark, doesn't reveal moments left
on the cutting room floor
as trees' detritus rustles beneath our feet
on a hot afternoon. Dawn will be cool, maybe even cold
if not tomorrow then the day after or a month later
when the season's gone and these pages bound.
In Montana or Montreal or somewhere else
they're cutting loose against the decay in their bones;
I'm looking to move to Fargo where floods
come with biblical regularity but no one has an ark —
all the cubits have been used up. There might be a quark
or two around, particles stranger than we strangers
struggling through words on this walk
along the garden's grassy paths bordered by plants
cultivated for reasons known and unknown.
There's no admission charge; but staying has a cost
and the exit is hard.

Frost

Perfect trees stand against the winter breeze;
frozen steps stretch across encroaching gloom
far from sunlit days and past evening's ease
while deep space reveals expanding rooms

that measure insignificance. You know
his neighbor's woods, the wall he didn't admire;
but in his meter's endless blow by blow
each footfall's cadence is forever mired

as on the tundra a lone elk's tracks
remain until the driven drifts expunge
all history, all knowledge, and the masks
truth wears, deceiving both old and young,

sporting with us. In this simple play with words
a poet sings; perhaps a bard is heard.

Death

What's he got to worry about?
No one will get away
whether he comes for them tomorrow
or today. Yet why is it *he*?
Don't wives or daughters have parts to play
where toil and sorrow trouble everyone?
He doesn't pout,
going solo for many centuries
without, it seems, a friend.
He gives damned and blessed
equal opportunity, delivering them both,
serving two masters without reward.
He could win a MacArthur prize
or a Guggenheim like his chronicler Simic
if he had a fixed address,
perhaps get tenure if he wasn't loth
to stay in one place being the steward
of hopes, knowing he will put out their eyes,
fastened to fate, pinned to the wall
through tragedy or accident
without any malicious intent.
It's a role he plays well —
he comes but once for us. So do not dwell,

don't worry: ask, what about his wife?
Where did he find her – was she chosen
from the dead? Why is her lot domestic,
ironing his robes? Or is his couture
more in keeping with the times
as he goes about making news for obits,
something off the rack at Saks or tailored
for the scene he's in, perhaps black leather,
a designer name you'd find in Vogue?
This woman, what of her life?
Did he take it before or after he took her?
Death in life, life in death, is that all?
Imagine his daughters' fury, setting supper
not knowing when he will return, what orbits
he spins spreading ruin in every culture
because his nature is rogue,
turning what is to what is not whether
through age, barbiturates, or vodka and lime.

He's compulsive about work; he has tics.
His ever-widening circle of friends
is no surprise to those who know him;
though he takes some on a whim
he's our constant companion when we reach the end.

The Hollow Hills

Please don't be mine for the taking:
life comes so easy, leaves so hard.
Every day I love living more
though it's only a habit:
familiar, comfortable, shameless.

I who cheat death with each day's laugh
want to laugh beyond the grave,
the mysterious wound which none survive.
Yet my words might, or my echo,
shadow of a voice that itself was shadow,
come back from the hollow hills
full of itself.

Walking About

I was on the road stretching
along a coast of affluence;
in the house with the tower
near the Franciscan priory
I saw my library in the garret
above the lake where bluffs defeat waves,
ravines of childhood opening onto the shore.
White washed stone and brick, a reliquary
with a cobbled courtyard past the arch;
I imagined a great reception hall
the slow climb up a garrulous staircase
the lake whispering at night
conversing with trees
lit by full moons,
the gas lamp's lingering light
weaving into shadows,
the eyes of those nearby
disappearing beneath the heavy-lidded brow of
darkness.
Somewhere on the shelves at the tower's top
high up, beyond reach, is a book
with my name on it. A relic of my library
filled with figures only dreams reveal,

pictures greeting the sleepy eye,
wishes that lie along the path
like fallen acorns or chestnuts before the blight.
The collection I gave away
lost when I abandoned writing,
when my voice quieter than a dead alewife
washed up on the beach among driftwood.
In that tower a prisoner reads.
Light bleeds through the long window;
falls like snow on the woods
hissing on the streetlamps,
snowflakes twinkling like diamonds
memorable for their mystery.
What was that to a young boy roaming,
finding secluded spaces and sequestered people
whose unknown minds troubling out the meanings
of texts and manuscripts meant so much?
While schoolchildren ducked under desks
fearing the hot winds of the cold war
I resolved to reach the bluffs, watch the closing show,
that furious lake steaming, fireballs colliding
leaves curling, crisping, flaming in their last fall
imagining man's descent into a disbeliever's hell
more profanely real than any sacred prophesy.
Each heartbeat a paragraph
in a different story than yet told,
each step marking a line along this trace

punctuated by scuffling stones in the gutter
where pavement yields to turning leaves
the wind stirring solitude, blue notes
atop my crenellated tower with an open book
beginning something great.

Interstices

In the garden between dawn and sunrise
there was laughter, the hour
between childhood and grief.
(Then I did not know
the next hour would make me old.)
My mother said "It's only fun the first time."
"So why did you have four kids?"
"You got me there."
I'm so deep in shame
there is no exit,
nor is salvation at hand:
Christ is not my friend, though he might befriend me:
belief, far beyond my capability
even if I wanted it sounds bitter.

Statement

I have had the drugs, the schools, the women and the
whores, cars, fashions, and the rage,
pleasures large wallets buy in every age;
I've sought forgetfulness, liquors from stygian springs
found where ferries link our shores
to those where none are more.
The ferryman's a friend; when I wish my end
he smiles and says – "You're not ready for this ride,
but soon you'll be as all before you are.
Give up suffering.
Iniquity's pleasures are for the damned:
living is for the living to command."

In that poetic past I sampled every sin
knowing the implacable would never let me win;
I fought and played, loved and betrayed,
possessed the best I could obtain —
I would, I think, do it all again.

Paul Muldoon Ends Poetry

There's a fellow I could like:
overstudious but puckish
perhaps a bit full of himself
a three-keyboard organ all stops out
working the pedals while Zevon
cranks it in the background
and the OED lies open to some weird word
he thinks it important we know.

With the blessings of Heaney
and the fealty of fellows
Oxford's gate admitted him to sit
where Auden sat and Padel fucked up
after Eliot elevated theft to high art
making pretence a virtue
turning the obscure into a mark of authority
just as I do. "Do as I do
if you dare" every strong poet says -
it's not so easy working a taut line
man on wire between twin towers
living and dying, imagination and wish
between hors d'oeuvres and the nightcap
a solitary fool takes as solace

when the muse has slipped away
with some Greek hero, a scholar of antiquity
or that rude boy who will ravish her
in an excitable way.

At Chicago changes ring from Mitchell tower
every Sunday. A New Yorker might not know
that but Oxford's bells call
unceasingly for those who care to listen.
Muldoon would know; I'll ask him
over sherry or port or pilsner, some poetic *dégustation*
when we distill the sounds of silence -
perhaps an absinthe
while pondering Cuchulain's battle with the sea
or tiresome neo-nazi graffiti.

Yes, Muldoon would know
the end of the poem is poetry's end
a life unlived like fruit fallen from a tree
or strangely hung by critics
lynching lines with white-out
sweeping uncouth words from the page
to preserve the litanies of literature.

The Tennessee Valley Authority

Orion lies prostrate in the sky;
His dagger rests against his thigh.
Here in Franklin lies no soul:
Imagination alone makes us whole.
Owls hide in this wilderness.
I knew when young the beautiful abyss –
Rome's canon draped it in a cassock
Only science could tear back.
Risible mists coronate the moon,
Silvered light gilds the leaves of youth.
Then I did not know
The next hour would make me old.

Sunset In 4.5

So Dennis Hopper's gone. It wasn't an easy ride.

Yeah man, it was tough watching him blown away. The
movie started with a sunset, exposed freedom's dangers
and ended with the admission: we blew it.

Peter Mareneck's gone too, but he rode a Harley once.
Taking Carli around the country until they found good
water and green woods in sweet springs. Now what we
have left of him is family, friends, and buildings he
made. I imagine marrying her, but she's already buried
one man, why should she bury two?

Linda Gregerson in Varenna sketched a sky in
watercolors rising and washing into the page of her mind
a sight free of time, light's river flowing through air.

Peter Jensen watched sunrise over Lake Michigan
climbing from recumbent darkness, lapping at the shore,
reminding us - for most there's an edge to night called
dawn.

It's the moonlight above her bed I remember, her
husband gone, their son asleep in the other room, her
teeth gleaming with stifled screams, hard-suckled
nipples bruised and sweating.

Hubble shows us not sunrise or sunset but stars forging a
luminous universe, each beacon a smithy's coal. We
pound ore into shape and call it wrought iron, reality, or
something like that. Freedom dies in Easy Rider and
dreams die too. There must be a reason the sunset is at
the beginning of the film. Near the end of the trip an
unremitting sun illuminates death, traced not by its
movement but by ours - sunrise sunset color beauty –
fabrications serving one purpose or another.

It was odd to hear bells at daylight tolling from an
orphaned belfry, remnants surviving a fascist regime,
ruins standing over an old village as a marriage began to
fail, livestock lowing beneath ancient apartments,
domiciled and domesticated as I could not be.

Every day billions of sunsets never seen again expire as
breath lost like the wind moving past, disturbing another
memory. We look, perhaps we see. We watch, perhaps
we know. We touch, perhaps we feel. The world knows
nothing of that, nor do we until we shape impressions
into words.

Easy Rider is a trip man, a trip many took from which few returned. You dig?

Psalm of the Lords

"When I stop by The Good Intent I drown sorrow before bedding down." - Lord Puttenham quoting Lord Denby

I lost my laugh when I met funny girl,
my fuck when I met Dulcinea,
yet I've laughed and screwed around
a lifetime. I touched the hand of Ibrahim Ferrer,
Ay Candela, Candela, listening to my man
bending gender though I've wanted a woman
singing songs for me all my life,
meeting in the middle;
that not possible, found domination
and women who went with it.
Now the middle is so near and far
that fantasy seems enough
for the hours and days remaining.

My song sung in earth's language
translates on every tongue:
love's desire, the final stanza, release and fulfillment,
lamentations of woman, furrows plowed
in endless cadenzas of seeding and harvest,
plaint and refrain weaving the tapestry
one sees from the air in flight.

My sons are the apostrophes of tongues,
rivers winding past windbreaks
levees on a road from somewhere to elsewhere,
through the heaving hills
a chorus of mountains above and below sea
drowning the solo voice inevitably arisen.

Before bedding down be of good intent:
Thus saith the lords.

His Mother and Mine

Years ago Strand wrote about his mother.
She, now dead, predisposed his melancholy
To find in the dim hour's light
The cinders of heaven burning out
As he struggled to make peace with time.
Little was left of origins
And less of futures in that gray expanse
Where silent currents escaped beneath the waves
And moonlight draped itself over land and sea.

My mother lives still, shrouded like his
In veils of cigarette smoke
The unspoken past
Wafting like an idle imp about her children
Ready to make sport of them.

I don't know Mark nor has he any idea
That I am the next to flail after him
Seeking voice for the music of wings
Or meaning for the eruptions
That bring celestial temperatures to earth,
Incinerating hope and filling the sky with ash.
Late is now an overused word, but in the night

When I forget day's failure
The remembrance of dawn draws me on.

Poetry

. . . I found her, beautiful but slovenly,
made up with the cheap rhetoric of Madison Avenue
wearing the parlous décolletage of confessional politics
in the wake of a scandal. She would fight, sometimes,
eager to be a bondage-slut for public indignation,
and only after I pleased her wanton
would I take her home and love her until sleep overcame us.

Since our first romance I've watched her
having a fling with the conversational, those countless courtiers
imagining they could seize and make her theirs,
sometimes to great acclaim, the parlor tricks
of poets laureate and committees
singing her praise. Singing, as though they and the sirens
could make a song so sweet none could resist
even in myth, overcoming all misprision
and making the world new.

Thousands declaim her, supplicants
seeking favors whose luscious gardens they enjoy
while fortune gives her gilded smile.
I name none: rather go into the gutter to retrieve her
I abandoned years ago, rejected by that namesake

whose pageant and beauty was the last call of the idyll
and my sibyl's curse. Signs of success passing
directions to streetwalkers and drivers alike
tower over us as they make their way. We lie in vomit,
full of disgust, remnants of a late night when civility
shattered as a wedding glass
broke the oath
Her eyes smoldering like an angry Norse goddess.

She was beautiful, I remember; and I, hollowed out
By the toothless old hag who ate my entrails
Still pursue her.

Tapestry

I am the prisoner of these words
you know nothing else of me
what's said here leads to wonder.
If you have certainty
you are one step ahead of me;
clearly I mean something
but saying the leaves are green,
what does that portend?
That they're beginning of the season, new buds —
or fulsome in summer, or they remain
green as they reach their fall descent?
The car going by - is it just passing my wandering eye
or do I see someone going where they need to go?

I'm the prisoner of these words.
You are imprisoned too
the judge and jury, as my friend Derek says,
is you and you and you and you
readers and critics joined together, lovers of the word
prisoners of the phrase
hostages to tropes weaving and binding them
ivies climbing the parapets
surrounding those imposing traditional windows
where Rapunzel let down her hair,

Romeo wooed Juliet
or some such nonsense
while in the library the tutor taught you
words that take hostages
holding what I said and what we think I meant
in the same valence. What tapestries are these?

Love Song to the Factory Poem

I have heard them, their reading
with slightly asthmatic rheumatic rhythms
of a poem from influence, a poem laid out on the page
whose cadence is regular as the sutures of a surgeon
closing a crooked wound, while in the gallery above,
below those bright lights students observe
thinking of stitching their own lines together
to make new poems that sound the same
no matter what they say.

I have heard them sing like this,
the rasp of a needle on an old record
at the end of its arc,
scratching that oblique silence
unknown to those beyond vinyl,
whose music comes through iTunes or MP3s
or colleagues in the academies.

I have seen them, lines rustling
across the page like evergreens in winter
or bare boughs under the gray-skied expanse
where experience of clouds paints dull monochromes
from horizon to horizon, each rising vowel sinking back
to the soft consonance of earth. Now,

I have scrawled them, prescriptions
mostly therapeutic, narcotic illusions
in verse, in tones illegible,
metaphors indifferent to any other
yet clamoring to be unique, dreams
against the eyelids, stretched out in the dark,
accompanied by the inner voice forgotten when we wake;
and now I've spoken them, and you have heard
about the end of the poem, the beginning of the word.

Pastiche

We put it all together,
        snips, stitches, lost cuttings

A snapshot will do. Porträt des jungen Goethe
        in Rom, in Basel leb' ich
also, Haydn wrote for the Esterhazys

I have no patron but the public
        (poetry from Gödel (v. Escher and Bach),
Lehninger's molecular logic
                          they report to me
events they think important

Were I an anaesthetist
I could earn SR 240,000 p.a. ("You will have had
experience . . .")

For years I sought turbulence,
a drunken boat on rivers breaking banks,
my voyage impossible to see, tormented rains
expressing overburdened clouds, not in trousers

The French legation pulled poetry from the salon
(where, prettily withered, were replicated manners

and grace), made a charnel-house thrust—

Then Eliot's preciosity, Pound's pomposity
bantered about the angst of trying to know it all:
'Yet must thou sail after knowledge,'
'After such knowledge, what forgiveness?'

Tous les maîtres sont morts.

                              Today's response,
poetry like paper-mache

                    concrete idiosyncracies
cemented in fabrics of sensibility.

What we have needs cachet. We admire the Tuileries
When not thinking about the possibilités Pigalle.
Ooh-la-la (gustatory verse from the gestes) kiss me
Madeline, Claudine, Marie! Love's arrow
        draws through our loins,
stylus and slate brailling away.

Thin Strand

With two quick strokes
My strophe ended:
My verse over
I sank to earth again,
That tenuous moment
Suspended
Between twin darknesses.

Xerxes In The Book of Esther

No woman comes unbidden to my sight
without risking life. Yet the cause you plead,
unlike my former queen, makes no demands
for gain against my royal right. You deign

Grace greater than my kingdom's light
to bear; fealty to me did not lead
you in. Your wishes my whim commands-
my edicts in your hands, I give you reign

To make me as just a man as woman might.
Though king, overmastered I yield: what's decreed
may not be undone throughout my lands
save by you, for whose love I will not feign

To be more than what I seem to be:
humbled regarding your civility.

Sound Bites

"Jon Welsh, a poet whose voice captured popular and academic audiences alike died yesterday at 8:59 pm. He was known for revealing lines that in a few words left us delighted, wondering, or perplexed.

A prolific blogger on politics, culture and society who also wrote books, essays, songs and screenplays, he lived his belief that artists have social responsibilities and that art for art's sake is just, as he put it, a nocturnal emission.

His poems encompassed romance, science, metaphysics and politics with wry views of human foibles, often expressed in his mordant optimism.

Jon Welsh was 95.

Here, now, are some of his words, with brief thematic prefaces ...

At 18, following a deep crisis and despairing of hopes for poetry, he burned all his youthful works and took up studies of mysticism and eastern religions. He immersed himself in the Tao Te Ching and summarized it for Western readers

reversal is the way
my silence speaks
when you listen
and you hear

At 30, with intimations of mortality, speaking of his youthful boasts he said

Then I did not know
The next hour would make me old

*He had a tumultuous love life with several marriages and
numerous affairs, of which he sometimes spoke quite
poignantly:*

Our past an archipelago of possibilities
Quenched where fire and water met
- -

A morning I have ridden toward
For thirty years
- -

Finding no legs parted for mine alone
I made figures of imagination
More beautiful and bitter than the rest
- -

Your silence, your absence
Your violin's bow poised above the strings
Before the cadenza.
- -

There to do what no law can
Nor government nor family deny,
To stand and banish time and death
We'll meet on Gretna Green.

*He often commented on our place in the universe and
power in relationships:*

deep space reveals expanding rooms
That measure insignificance.
- -

Every pantheon has a litany of fools
that foil and fox the great.
- -

Though king, overmastered I yield . . . .
I will not feign . . .
to be more than what I seem to be:
Humbled regarding your civility.
- -

Each hour marks the progress of the race, the long
lapse
between promise and justice and peace.
- -

in the elusive sands of rhyme
each apparition walks back in time.
- -

When I forget day's failure
the remembrance of dawn draws me on.

Sometimes he just painted a picture:

in small towns where not much happens,
where everything happens to be forgotten
a train's whistle dapples the wind
rising and fading away.

In rejecting a love affair he said

I move away
unwilling to be the hunter
or the prey.

Of his own checkered history he observed

I have had the drugs, the schools, the women and the whores,
the cars, the fashions and the rage,
pleasures large wallets buy in every age;
iniquity's pleasures are for the damned -
living is for the living to command."

He had a lifelong love of wine and cognac and wrote:

This sad café
where I drink alone
calls me to other lands.

Returning to the theme of love relations and his lifelong memories of loves and love affairs reflected against our common fate, he looked to the future with both questions and acceptance.

Can you tell whose dance you danced?
- -

I have seen my resting-place taken away
and wonder what archeologist will dig
this vase, once repository of a soul,
now an instrument of emptiness.
- -

Eternal mornings await our effortless arrival;
experience laughter
and wry approval of disappointment.

Jon Welsh often urged his fellow poets to merge private and public moments in verse, and was skeptical about academic claims on poetry and poetry that remained in the personal:

I don't know Mark [Strand] nor has he any idea
that I am the next to flail after him
seeking voice for the music of wings
or meaning for the eruptions
that bring celestial temperatures to earth,
incinerating hope and filling the sky with ash.
- -

[professors] eyes
scan the steps before them lest they slip and fall,
bearing poetry dead among us all.

*And in the prescience of his own claim to be a great poet
he set down these lines:*

I stand in shoals
impatient for a boat
- -

I know the number of the world's wishes
but the counting of tears escapes me
- -

those who live
endlessly no longer seek cafés for idle conversation
but a banquet with voices from the past.
We are not far from pretense;
I write with a golden pen.
- -

Each syllable a beat of blood
each heartbeat a paragraph
beginning something great.

*And finally, of his beloved Poetry, who outlasted his many
careers, marriages, travels and the circumstances of a life
that biographers will now start revealing for his readers*

*and graduate students, we leave you with his words about
the Muse that he revered all his life:*

She was beautiful, I remember, and I, hollowed out
by the toothless old hag who ate my entrails
still pursue her.

Weibo II

If only I were Chinese.
Then I wouldn't have to write at all,
because everything I wrote would be censored.
Perhaps if I dreamed I were Chinese,
I could write what I would say
knowing that no one would ever read it.
Then I would be a great writer.

NOTES

Simplicity – Inspired by reading *"On the Relationship Between Poetry and Joke-telling by David Yezzi"* in *Contemporary Poetry Review.*

A Life in the Day - NY Times Archive for January 30, 1969.

A Vacant God's So Torn - anagram of Avogadro's constant.

Antidote to Frank O'Hara's Excitement - Wayne Koestenbaum's " *'Oh! Kangaroos, Sequins, Chocolate Sodas!'*: Frank O'Hara's *Excitement*" in Poet – Journal of the American Academy of Poets, v39, Fall 2010.

Bobby Bringhurst Talks to a Frog – Robert Bringhurst addressing the Library of Congress on April 21, 2011, upon winning the Witter Bynner Award, awarded that year by W.S. Merwin.

Dear Reader – *"Black Mountain Days"* by Michael Rumaker.

Death – Charles Simic's *"Eyes Fastened With Pins."*

Digital Nomad - Poems on the wall: Reba McEntire's *"This Picture."* Azure (Microsoft); Amazon S3. John Fowles. Those days: those were the days (my friend, we thought....). Long since forgotten: now forgotten. Subway walls and tenement halls (Simon and Garfunkel). Bit: byte: word. Fab four (Beatles) (All You Need Is Love; Lennon's remark about Christ). No end to beginning: Eliot.

Ellen's Grief - After a reading by Ellen Bass at the Library of Congress, April 28, 2009.

Fire, Air, Earth, Water – Reading about and by Wallace Stevens on the anniversary of his birthday, Oct. 2, 1879. Also, James Wood's New Yorker review ("Desert Storm") of James Alters's new translation of *The Book of Psalms*.

Frost - Perfect trees: Frost's *"A Prayer In Spring."* Other Frost: *"The Host Follower"* *"A Microscopic Speck"* *"A Gift Outright"* *"To A Thinker"* and the usual old chestnuts.

His Mother and Mine – Mark Strand's *"My Mother on an Evening in Late Summer."*

Hospice – In memoriam, Sue Peters Carlson (January 2, 1952 – January 22, 2011).

Interstices – James Branch Cabell's *"Jurgen."* Brian Desmond's *"Bicycles."* My own *"Tennessee Valley Authority."* Mother. Sartre. Salvation advocates and atheists.

Kay's Crystals – Kay Ryan's readings as U.S. Poet Laureate at the Library of Congress.

Montage: Wolf Kahn's Landscape – On seeing an exhibition of his works at Cheekwood Art & Gardens in Nashville, Tennessee, in 1982.

Music In The Night – The foreshadowing of my epic: "that later will describe an epoch/when one voice claims it as its own,/defining a time for all times/sowing a seed that once sown/will last and outlast the moment of its birth." If I don't live to write it, the ambition stands.

Nemerov Rewritten – See Howard Nemerov's *"Writing."*

Paul Muldoon Ends Poetry – See Paul Muldoon's "The End of Poetry." ". . . tiresome neo-nazi graffiti" refers to an incident at Princeton. Billie Holliday: Strange Fruit. Rude boy… excitable way: Warren Zevon's "Excitable Boy." And how can one think of strong poetry without Harold Bloom?

Procrastination - James Surowiecki's New Yorker article on procrastination.

Psalm Of The Lords - Ay Candela – Buena Vista Social Club / Ibrahim Ferrer. Puttenham, England; Lord Denby in "The Black Swan."

The Tennessee Valley Authority – Written in Franklin, Tennessee, November, 1981.

Weibo I – From a New York Times article (July 29, 2011) on Chinese blogs and tweeting (tweeting = knitting; in Chinese the word "weibo" also means scarf) "Their [leaders] names become our history, while ours live with those we knew." There are always screenshots to preserve posts that are deleted, such as this one by Ge You, one of China's most distinguished actors: "If a higher-level leader died," he wrote, "there would be countless wreaths; however, when many ordinary people died, there was only endless harmony" — a euphemism for censorship. "If a higher-level leader died, there would be nationwide mourning; however, when many ordinary people died, there was not a single word of apology. If a higher-level leader died, there would be high-end funerals; however, when many ordinary people died, there were only cold numbers."

Xerxes In The Book Of Esther – The biblical story told again, in the King's voice.